Dinner for God Planner

By

RAYME SCIARONI

MW01630160

Copyright © 2013 by Rayme Sciaroni

Publishing Unleashed

All rights reserved. No part of this publication may be reproduced,
stored in a retrieval system, or transmitted in any form or any
other means electronic, mechanical, photocopying, recording or oth-
erwise, without the prior written permission of the publisher.

www.publishingunleashed.com

ISBN-13: 978-0-9850931-8-1

Library of Congress Control Number: 2013907335

Manufactured in the United States of America

Publishing Unleashed
10449 Leslie Drive
Raleigh, North Carolina 27615

Dedication

I dedicate this book to a very special man in my life.

His diligence and forethought in all of his endeavors only enhances my own.

His attention to detail when planning any kind of event; whether it's arranging a trip or scheduling a special occasion with family and friends, he continuously teaches and reminds me how important and heart felt that even the smallest detail can and should be.

I am grateful for him and I honor his generous Soul in All Ways.

My partner and best friend,
Steven Charles Gardepie.

Welcome!

Everything you need to think about for planning and making your very own Dinner for God are in these pages. Of course, if you're familiar with how to create a special dinner party, this planner can only enhance how special you want to make your event. You have decided that it will be a dinner party like no other dinner party! The stakes have been raised. The quest for high quality and detail, right down to the smallest sugar cube, cannot be overlooked.

But, is putting on a Dinner for God a chore? Do you think that putting on a dinner party is a chore? Ah! Thus, the difference! Because of the special qualities you are choosing to bring to your table, you declare this entire journey as a fun and joyful one—one that you'll want to repeat over and over again, and one that you can encourage others to do for their families and friends. You are at the helm of inspiring others through your choice of colors, plates, flatware, invited guests, discussion topics—all with your connection to your God or Highest Source! (Choose the name that best suits you and your loved ones. To avoid confusion, I will continue to use the word "God" for your event, but you have the freedom to make the word "God" more personal and spiritual to you.)

Let's be bold together, dear Host or Hostess of God! Let's put our absolute best thoughts forward in creating this grand event in *your* very own house, or yard, or rooftop!

Remember this:

When we are shining at our brightest and giving of ourselves from our brightest, it is infectious. How could anyone NOT want to be involved? And... the ones who don't wish to participate with you are the ones who are not meant to be at this particular Dinner. (Maybe they'll come around when you have your next Dinner for God...or perhaps your Brunch for God!)
Let's get started...and LOVE the *Journey*!!!

I remember clearly having lunch by myself in my dining room one day when a question came to my mind:

If God were coming to my house for dinner, what would I serve?

I dropped my fork onto my plate because this felt rather important at that moment. And then a flood of questions followed:

What would I serve?

What would I wear?

Whom would I invite?

What would we talk about?

What should the food be served on?

Which dinner plates, napkins, and silverware should I use?

What kind of tablecloth?

What about candles?

These questions and more came at me so suddenly that I didn't know where to begin! But the underlying feeling of it was exciting and new. That's what got my attention, and I knew that I had to discover and create it.

These questions may be as overwhelming for you as they were for me. Coming up with a planner to make it easier seemed the best way to handle such a task. When you can break everything down step by step, it doesn't seem as mountainous and impossible. And why should it be? It's God, after all! God knows us and loves us unconditionally, so there's not going to be a "wrong" way to have a Dinner for God!

The only difference between this dinner and any other dinner you have planned is the way you start, from the very beginning, *knowing* that you will be preparing dinner for a Higher Power. You must remember to tune into your Highest Self at all times. That's what makes this the special evening that it's meant to be.

So, here is where I ask *YOU* the first question that I asked myself:

*If God were coming to your house for
dinner, what would you serve?*

From here, we will go through each step of what needs to be done and in what order. There are plenty of blank pages provided so that you can keep notes on what has been accomplished and what needs your attention. I've also provided extra blank pages so that you can share your thoughts and experiences as you move from step to step. This is key. That is why this book is more than a planning guide—it is also a journal that can be used for your "sacred thoughts." Make this your own book! Include funny anecdotes or anything that feels "God-like," special, or profound. Write it in here. It's all part of the grand experience—not only for yourself but also for those with whom you choose to share this special night.

Back to the first question:

If God were coming to my house for dinner, what would I serve?

The reason I like starting with this question is because, as the host, I give myself permission to make the first choice of what I would want to serve to God. If you're into cooking like me, even on a small scale, you will no doubt have several recipes that you would be more than proud to serve. (Just another reason for you to have MORE meals for God and make a different great dish for each event!)

Write it here. What dish would you like for God to taste? Give this some thought. It doesn't have to be the most difficult dish that you can prepare, nor does it have to contain the most exotic of ingredients. The dish that *YOU* love to make, love to share, and that people always rave about when you make it might be the perfect choice. I would suggest that this dish be one with which you are very familiar...one that you have perfected more and more each time you've made it, and one that has your distinct flavor.

My dish for God: ____

I have chosen this dish because: __________________________________

____

Pick a date. Easy enough, yes? Maybe. Make sure, of course, that the chosen date is picked well in advance so that your invited guests are sure to attend. I encourage you to pick a date that doesn't necessarily have any significant meaning. However, you should choose a date other than a birthday, anniversary, or any other date that would normally be celebrated. Although there are no rules in terms of picking a date, there may be a date that is extremely personal and noteworthy for you, which you would like for God to celebrate with you. (Maybe it's a "secret" date that only you and God share.) For me personally, the idea of an anonymous date reminds my guests and myself that every day and every meal should be (and IS) a "God" day and a "God" meal.

("Good" day, "Good" meal = "God" day, "God" meal. Hmmm.)

Also, decide what time your dinner should begin. Will it be when the sun has set? Will it be before the sun has set? Maybe you want the dinner to start when it is already dark. Determine your favorite time of the evening and begin your special night at that time.

Write your preferred date and time for your Dinner for God here and a few sentences on why this date and time was your personal pick.

My Dinner for God Date: ______________________________________

I chose this date because: ____________________________________

____

____

My Dinner for God Time:

I chose this time because:

Whom do you wish to invite to a Dinner for God? Who do you love and trust enough to share this important Grand Evening with? Who will contribute to and benefit from this High and Joyful event?

How many people will you invite? What is manageable for you? Don't feel the need to go over-board with this. If it is a table for four people, or twelve, or beyond, do what is comfortable for you.

Be clear within yourself about whom you are inviting and why you are inviting them. Make sure your guest list is everyone that you *want* to have. Don't make it a meal where you are inviting someone out of guilt or obligation. Make this a "true to your heart" dinner. Treat it as the most important gathering you will ever have. God is worth it... YOU are worth it!

Write your guest list here, and after each name, write a short sentence on why you want them to be at this Dinner for God.

Guest #1:

Why I want them at my Dinner for God:

Guest #2:

Why I want them at my Dinner for God:

Guest #3: ____

Why I want them at my Dinner for God: ___________________

____

Guest #4: ____

Why I want them at my Dinner for God: ___________________

____

Guest #5: ____

Why I want them at my Dinner for God: ___________________

____

Guest #6: ____

Why I want them at my Dinner for God: ___________________

____

Guest #7: ____

Why I want them at my Dinner for God: ___________________

____

Guest #8: ____

Why I want them at my Dinner for God: ______________

____

Guest #9: ____

Why I want them at my Dinner for God: ______________

____

Guest #10: ____

Why I want them at my Dinner for God: ______________

____

Guest #11: ____

Why I want them at my Dinner for God: ______________

____

Guest #12: ____

Why I want them at my Dinner for God: ______________

____

Whoa! Why am I asking this now and not earlier?!

Think of how far you've already come. The idea of putting on a "Dinner for God" is exciting! Feel the energy that you've collected while doing the first steps of planning for it. My guess is that it's exhilarating to be creating something like this!

It's new! It's joyful! You want to be a part of something important that involves a heart-felt experience for you and your loved ones!

I want you to revel in these emotions for yourself. It IS fun!
But be prepared with an answer when your guests ask you, "Why are you having a Dinner for God?"

Think of all of the reasons that come to you as you write down and create your answer...not only for your invited guests but for yourself as well.

The answer that comes up for you is the *right* answer for the people you want to invite. You will undoubtedly be asked, so help clarify for yourself by writing answers to the three questions found on the following pages.

Why do I want to host a "Dinner for God"?

What would I like for my guests to experience?

What would I like for myself to experience?

~ 13 ~

How will you invite your chosen guests? Will you do it on the phone? Will you e-mail them? Will you send them a mailed invitation? Will you ask them in person? How would you prefer to go about inviting people to such an extraordinary event? What is the best way to invite them that is important enough for you and will convey its importance to your guests?

If you decide to tell them by phone or in person, how will you approach the subject? Just remember to keep it light and fun.
Being direct is always a good idea, too! Here's an example of what you might say:

"Listen, God's coming to my house for dinner on (date here) at (time here), and I would love it if you could come, too."

Undoubtedly you will get smiles and giggles before you have to go on and explain what your intent is and why you are doing it. Don't hold back. Share openly with your guests and let them see, hear, and feel the "heart truth" behind your words.

If you choose to send a mailed invitation to possible guests, you may use the worded invitation below. You may copy it onto your computer and choose an elegant font of your choice, then print it on elegant paper.

Invitation #1

Dear _____________________,

God will be dining at my house for dinner on (<u>date</u>) at (<u>time</u>).

Your presence is requested in joining Us for this distinguished occasion.

You have the opportunity to prepare a dish that you would like for God to taste, and to dress in your finest clothing, which you would like for God to see you wearing.

You are further invited to bring with you something special of yourself that you would like to share with God and the other guests. This may be in the form of a poem, a song, a story, etc.—something that comes directly from your heart that would be worthy to impart to God and the other guests.

The purpose of this joyous event is for a sharing of the Divine-ness that We are, and to perhaps remind us all in some small way how much We are greatly loved all the time, without end.

Please R.S.V.P. with your choice of dish to share with God by (<u>date here</u>).

(In YOUR handwriting, you may want to sign it:)

In Love,

(Your Signature)

OR....

Choose to have "God" send out the invitation:

Invitation #2

Dear _________________________,

One of my finest creations, (<u>your name</u>), will be hosting a dinner in My honor on (<u>date and time</u>) at (<u>address</u>).

(<u>Your name</u>) has requested you in joining Us for this distinguished occasion, and I am more than pleased.

You have the opportunity to prepare a dish that you would like for Me to taste, and to dress in your finest clothing, which you would like for Me to see you wearing.

You are further invited to bring with you something special of yourself that you would like to share with Me and the other guests. This may be in the form of a poem, a song, a story, etc.—something that comes directly from your heart that would be worthy to impart to Me and the other guests.

The purpose of this joyous event is for a sharing of the Divine-ness that We are, and to perhaps remind you in some small way how much You are greatly loved all the time, without end.

Please R.S.V.P. with your choice of dish to share by (<u>date here</u>).

I so look forward to Our Grand Sharing together.

In Love,

GOD

You may also go to www.dinnerforgod.com where these invitations already exist. You can copy and print them from there. Feel free to change the wording to suit your needs. Or, make up your very own invitation! It's YOUR Dinner for God!

Will you hand deliver them? (Perhaps sliding them under the doors of your chosen guests?)

Will you mail them by snail mail?

If so, what kind of envelope will you use?

What, to you, is "God-worthy" to send to your invitees?

OR

Will you pick a preferred font and e-mail your invitations?

Perhaps you can include a favorite photo of yours, which you can attach to the invitation. Or maybe a favorite border!

Play with this and see what feels right to you.

On the following pages, write down what you chose to say for your invitations and paste your envelope on the blank page provided.

My 'High Dinner' Invitation

My 'High Dinner' Invitation Envelope

The following pages are for your extra thoughts!

What has this been like so far for you?

What are your thoughts as each guest confirms whether they are coming (or not coming)?

How has their reaction and response been for the entire planning of this?

What kinds of conversations have you had with them about the event?

Give yourself the opportunity here to let all of your thoughts and ideas flow. Write down the funny or important little stories that have happened along the way, which has gotten you to this point.

Once everyone has confirmed and told you what dish they are bringing, round out the meal with what is necessary. If you have guests who first ask you what the meal may need—a salad, bread, etc.—ask them to supply that. You will undoubtedly have a guest or two who may want to contribute with a side dish that will accompany the rest of the dishes. Go ahead and let your guests know a portion of, or the entire menu so they can "tune in" to what the rest of the meal may need in order to be complete.

Write down the final menu here, as well as your thoughts on the collection of dishes, what will be served, and in what order.

The Dinner For God Menu:

My dish:

____

____

Guest 1:

____

____

Their chosen dish:

____

____

Guest 2:

____

____

Their chosen dish:

____

____

Guest 3:

____

____

Their chosen dish:

____

Guest 4: ____

____

Their chosen dish: ___________________________________

____

Guest 5: ____

____

Their chosen dish: ___________________________________

____

Guest 6: ____

____

Their chosen dish: ___________________________________

____

Guest 7: ____

____

Their chosen dish: ___________________________________

____

Guest 8: ____

____

Their chosen dish: ___________________________________

____

Guest 9: _______________________________

____

Their chosen dish: _______________________________

____

Guest 10: _______________________________

____

Their chosen dish: _______________________________

____

Guest 11: _______________________________

____

Their chosen dish: _______________________________

____

Guest 12: _______________________________

____

Their chosen dish: _______________________________

____

Side dishes that I will add: _______________________________

____

Okay! What is your table setting going to look like? Do you have a color scheme in mind? Do you want to use a tablecloth that you already have? Do you want several tablecloths to layer over each other, such as Jenny did in the story?

Much depends on how large your group is going to be and how big of an eating area you are going to need.

Write down your table setting here. Include the colors you have picked, tablecloth(s), your chosen plates, glasses, flatware, and general look. Write down why you have chosen this particular setting and what it means to you.

WHAT ELSE? Write down any extra things that you might want to have set up in order to make your dinner complete. Candles, flowers…maybe a small collection of items you may have that can be at the center of the table. An example would be a mix of different shapes and sizes of flower vases. If they are clear, you can fill them with colored marbles and water. ANYTHING that you decide to do will be RIGHT! Go "God" CRAZY here!

Celebrate this time, as you may have extra thoughts and ideas that you add to this. (Do you want fun, small dishes for holding salt and pepper?) If any dish needs a spice or a side sauce, what kind of unique bowl or plate will you serve it in? Write down all the details!

Place Cards! Do you want them? What kind of place cards do you want? Do you want to make them by hand with your handwriting? Maybe you know someone who has extraordinary handwriting or knows how to do calligraphy and can design your list of names for you. Go to your computer if you wish and pick a font and size, print them out on specialized paper, and glue them onto folded card stock. Get creative! Your place cards can be folded into odd triangular shapes...or maybe a variety of origami papers with names written on them will be the way you want to go. Paste the names on over-sized leaves from your garden! This kind of personal touch is what keeps it fun.

If you chose to do a place card, make an extra one and paste it here:

Where will each person sit and whom will they sit next to? Write down why you chose these seating arrangements for your guests.

As you are writing this, make sure you don't try to "control" the dinner. Look to "weave" other people's ideas and meal additions into a wonderful, flavorful, and eclectic occasion. Write down all of your thoughts about how this can be put together. Remember, God put a few BILLION very different people on this planet, no two alike, so don't try to go against that for your dinner. Let it flow!

And more importantly, keep your thoughts and your writings JOY-FULL! Don't let the fear in, because that is not a place where God would even want you to consider going to!

Who will sit next to whom and why?

What chair have you chosen for God's chair? Where will you place God's chair at your table? Will it be at one end? Will it be in the center of one side of your table between some of your guests?

I suggest putting the chair somewhere at the table where all of your guests can see it clearly. Some people may be inspired to speak directly to the chair as if "God" is sitting there.

What kind of chair do you think God would like to sit in at your table?

Pick a chair that you may already have, or if one of your guests has the perfect chair, go ahead and ask if you can borrow it! Does it need a soft cushion or two, or perhaps a lap blanket draped over the back? Maybe you have a swath of fabric that you can drape over the entire chair and tie at the back.

The chair I have chosen for God is

I chose this chair because:

Write down all of the things you need to do to prepare for this meal and organize it within a few days before the Dinner.

What grocery shopping do you need to do and when? Does anything have to thaw out before cooking? Will you be serving a "final delicacy," such as a blue M&M or similar for the "Final God Thoughts"? Give yourself enough time and thought for each errand that needs to be taken care of. You have been given enough room and designated times to write out your "Tasks of Joy"!

This is also a good time for you to think about what *you* will be sharing for the "God Sharing" part of the evening. Will you sing a song or recite a poem? Perhaps you are able to make a small craft project—one for each person. Figure out what that extra something is that you do and share it with your guests. It could be as easy as making copies of your invitation, with blank spaces where names should be so that your guests can create their own Dinners for God.

Following your line of "to do" lists, I also encourage you to start a "7 Days of Meditation" before your actual Dinner for God. These meditations don't have to be long. Find a certain time each day—anywhere from five to ten minutes—to sit with your eyes closed. Let your mind go blank, then whisper, "My Dinner for God." Meditate on that statement and let your inner-Being send your most loving intent outward for your dinner. Imagine "blanketing" your chosen area of dining with this energy. Let the feeling of joy, excitement, and love flow throughout yourself, throughout the whole of the evening. After each meditation, write down what came up for you.

7 DAYS BEFORE: Finish your shopping list? Does anything need to be pre-ordered? Confirm guests by phone? Check whether they are choosing to share something with your guests during the "God Sharing" portion of your evening and what it is they are sharing. (If they choose to do a dance, do you have the room for it, and will they need to use a music box device? If they need a keyboard, do you have one or will they bring their own?)

My 7th Day "Tasks of Joy" are

My 7th Day "Before Meditation" brought up for me:

My 6th Day "Tasks of Joy" are

5 DAYS BEFORE: Is your selected area for your dinner straightened up? (Vacuumed, dusted, arranged with plants, etc.?)

My 5th Day "Tasks of Joy" are

My 4th Day "Tasks of Joy" are

My 3rd Day "Tasks of Joy" are

2 DAYS BEFORE: Last minute items needed. Does the silver need to be polished?

My 2ⁿᵈ Day "Tasks of Joy" are

1 DAY BEFORE: Pull out items that will need to be organized for the next day. Candles and candle-holders? Flower vases? Place cards and seating arrangements? You may also need to iron tablecloths and napkins.

My One Day Before "Tasks of Joy" are

Write down your tasks in order of importance. Most importantly, keep yourself in a joy-full existence while doing so. Make an effort to remain calm about this event. Choose to keep the entire day light, carefree, and exciting. Even if unforeseen circumstances may alter your plan, choose now to *not* let it interfere with the flow of your Highest Self working creatively and joyfully throughout the day.

My "Day of the Dinner Tasks of Joy" are

Think carefully about your dining area's surroundings. Set not only your table in the theme you are intending but also the area around it. Do you have candles on your table? Do you want extra candles lit against the walls around the table? Perhaps twinkling lights?

If you've adorned your table with flowers and foliage, you may want to continue with that theme around the dining table as well. Perhaps you have large potted plants that can be up-lighted to give a soft glow around the table.

Are you using shiny glass crystals in your theme? Do you have extras that you would like to have hanging from your ceiling?

You can make the entire area your "God" area. Don't be afraid to make it a slice of *heaven*!

What about music? Will you have soft music playing in the background? What kind of music will you choose? Write down all of your ideas for creating ambiance here:

The surroundings I have chosen are:

I chose this music because:

It's here! The day of YOUR Dinner for God! You have checked and double-checked everything that needs to be done, and you have written down, in order, what you are going to do.

I would suggest you start the day with a simple meditation for yourself. Sit comfortably for a few moments with your eyes closed and let yourself get centered. Decide that *your* centered self is where you are going to start and *BE* for the entire day. Consciously *CHOOSE* the *BLISS* of the moment that you have created. *CHOOSE* to stay in that bliss all day long! Don't miss out on a moment of this for yourself. It is *JUST* as important, if not more so, than the Dinner itself!

Before you go any further, use the following pages of lines for your very last minute "Task of Joy" list.

HINT:

Keep this book and pen near you while you are happily putting together the details of this meal. No doubt a few things will suddenly pop into your head that you must make sure to do, and as they come up, write them down on the "Task of Joy" page.

Be aware of *all* of the senses that you are using while you are setting the table. *Notice* the texture of the tablecloth you have unfurled to cover your table. *Enjoy* the placing of your table runner as it rolls down to the other end. *Observe* the weight of the plates as you arrange them perfectly in front of each chair.

Have *fun* with your napkins by either folding them onto each plate, traditionally setting them to the left side of the plate, or perhaps have them uniquely folded and placed halfway off the plate. *Feel* the smoothness of each piece of silverware as you arrange them.

Set your table and create your environment. Set out your chair for God.

Take a picture of your table and paste it on the following blank page.

Pull out extra platters for the food your guests will be bringing.

Get ready! Take a shower or bath before the guests arrive! Put on your best clothes, your best jewelry, and perfume.

Your "best" doesn't have to be your most expensive. It's what you favor that makes you feel, look, and smell your best.

What you have chosen to wear? Don't leave any detail out. If you decide to use a fragrance, what will it be and why did you choose it?

Remember: *You don't have to go out and buy something new or extravagant for this dinner unless you want to. Take a good look in your closet and pick something that you know you look good and FEEL good in. No part of your outfit should feel the slightest bit uncomfortable.*

For my Dinner for God, I will be wearing: ______________________
____
____

I chose this out fit because: __________________________________
____
____

The shoes I will be wearing are: _______________________________
____
____

I chose these shoes because: __________________________________
____
____

The jewelry I have chosen is:

____

____

I chose this jewelry because:

____

____

The scent I have chosen is:

____

____

I chose this scent because:

____

____

I have added these accessories because:

____

____

Add a picture of you in your outfit on the following blank page.

Just before you are about to walk out of your dressing area, say a silent prayer asking the heavens to provide an extra blessing for the evening that is most certainly *already* blessed.

Start your personal silent prayer: *"Dear God ~ I am having a Dinner for You this evening. I have arranged everything to the best of my ability and ask for Your Joyful Presence to heighten the awareness of what already promises to be a very special night."* (Add additional thoughts of your own. You can write them down later.)

Now that you're looking *Highly-Holy Fabulous*, time for one last mental review before your guests arrive.

Fill the water glasses! Light the candles! Start the music!

Greet Your Guests

Your guests have arrived! Help them prepare their dishes so they, too, can be at their best presentation for the table. Have fun admiring each other's clothes, dishes, etc.

Take a picture of your guests and paste it on the following blank page.

Invite them to find their names on the place cards and take their seats.

You will notice that I do not have a segment here for appetizers and drinks before the dinner—and purposely so. For me, standing around holding a beverage and munching on small tidbits of goodies seems to take a good deal of meaning out of the evening. I like to keep the dinner focused as the most important aspect of the night. There will be plenty of food at the table, and I want my guests to fully explore and enjoy the flavors that are being served to them without filling up on appetizers before hand. You may feel differently and have created a "killer" appetizer that you simply must serve before the actual dinner. Go for it! It will work for you! Again, no set rules!

Have your guests who have prepared the first course set them onto the table.

You may now want to pour champagne or wine for each guest, if you have chosen any of these beverages. You might decide to ask a couple of your guests to help you pour around the table. You decide.

Ask your guests to please stand, hold their glasses, and acknowledge the chair for God—and that God is, in fact, sitting there. Let your guests look at the chair and create their own vision of what that may look like for them. Do the same for yourself.

You may want to say something like:

"Dearest friends and loved ones, I would like to thank you for coming to this very important and love-filled night. Our honored guest at the head of the table is God. You may have other names for Him or Her, and I invite you to take a moment, look at the chair, and envision what you consider your 'Highest Source' to look like for you—your most splendid and majestic notion of what you consider to be the most sacred energy for yourselves sitting in that chair. *That* is who we are dining with to-night. Allow this to be your truth."

Let a few moments of silence pass as you see your guests envisioning their version of God into the chair. When you feel that all have done so, raise your own glass to the "God" chair and say, "To God." Your guests will follow suit, and all will take a small sip from their glasses. Tell them that they may now take their seats.

As hostess/host, remain standing in respect for your guests until the last one has been seated. This also gives you time to provide your guests with silent thanks for their presence and envision your deepest truth of the High Energy you have placed in the chair.

Remember that for your guests, you are the link that holds the Dinner for God in its special place. You will be looked on for guidance on behavior and etiquette. Although you and your guests will naturally fall into an awareness of participating in a special and elegant evening, make sure to keep it light and fun. Make them feel comfortable being in such an environment, and make them feel that they are truly welcome and *deserve* to be there! Keep your idea of God casual, friendly, heartfelt, loving, and joyous. Your guests will feel the fun that you are having and will act accordingly. This is the reason to have such a meal. God would want you to be festive. Laugh! And if you are nervous, share that with your guests as well! Ask them if they are nervous! Break the ice any way you can think of so that all can be relaxed and centered in their connecting to the chair that God is sitting in.

A FUN TIP:

You may even take it so far as to have very small "finger bowls" in the center of each plate filled with a bit of water. Start by dipping your fingers into yours and flicking them at your guests and "blessing" them with the droplets of water that splash forward! Say BLESS as you do so! Encourage them to do the same and "bless" each other! Then have your guests and yourself simultaneously dip your fingers and flick them at God's chair to bless Him as well! Have fun with this! (And the cool droplets of water sprinkled around your guests and to God will be quite refreshing in more ways than one!)

Once everyone feels more relaxed, ask your guests to join hands for "grace." You may start, and you may say whatever you find in your heart that needs to be spoken. Trust yourself. Thank your guests for taking this journey with you. Thank God for showing up! Give a hint of what you expect to be brought forth for the evening, for a higher sense of spirit. This might include sharing different stories and ideas regarding each guest's version of God or how you look forward to learning about different aspects of The Universal connection we all share. Speak about how this is not an evening for heated debates or judgment on anyone else's beliefs. The evening is specifically designed for sharing, learning, and honoring the different ways we live our grandest of lives and to stay in the wonderment of the many different facets of who God is to each and every one of us. None of them are wrong, and all are sacred.

On the following page, you will find a sample of what "Grace" can be. Feel free to use any or all of it, and change any part of it that you wish. Print a copy and have it near your plate if you feel the need.

"Grace for God"

Dear God (Universe, High Source, etc.):

We are gathered here tonight with You to celebrate and honor the goodness that You are and the goodness that We are.

The most delicious food has been prepared for You, with the highest integrity. We have dressed in a manner that presents our Highest Selves to You.

We ask that tonight's sharing with You stay within the deepest part of our hearts without judgment, and to actively make a conscious choice to rejoice in our differences and views of You.

We are One and the Same.

Bless.

*(This "Grace" can be copied from the website
www.dinnerforgod.com under "Free Inspiration.")*

Invite each guest who prepared a dish for the evening to introduce it. Let them share what dish they made and why they chose to make it for this special occasion.

Pass the dishes around and dig in!

You might ask your guests to put themselves in a "High Place of Consciousness" as to the flavor of what they are eating.

Remind them that the finest of foods have been prepared with the finest ingredients to be enjoyed with the finest company. Remind them to notice the enticing flavors that are coming from that place of thought and Being.

As you and your guests are enjoying the delectable meal, there are many special topics—both fun and insightful—which you might explore together. For you as the host, be prepared to start the conversation with this in mind.

You might start out with simple and fun questions for your guests to answer...just be prepared to answer the same questions you ask! Your guests may pick up on where you are steering the conversation and ask questions of their own to share at the table. However the talk goes, it's bound to be entertaining and inspiring.

Here are a few topic questions that you may use to start things off:

- ❖ What is your word for God?

- ❖ What does Heaven look like?

- ❖ What would you want to tell God about yourself?

- ❖ What would you want to ask God, and how do you think God would answer?

- ❖ What would you do if YOU were God?

- ❖ Share your own personal God moment, or "miracle" that has no logical explanation.

- ❖ What is your grandest wish for yourself?

❖   What is your highest wish for the world?

❖   If YOU were God, what is the message that you would want to give to the world?

❖   Name one favorite item for each of the senses:

- Sight – What is your favorite sight to look at?
- Sound – What is your favorite sound to hear?
- Touch – What is your favorite thing to physically feel?
- Taste – What is your favorite flavor?
- Smell – What is your favorite fragrance?

❖   Name a favorite feeling and why.

❖   Share a favorite quality that you love about someone.

❖   In <u>two words only</u>, what is your *true* desire for Being here on this planet. Examples: "Touch Hearts," "Spread Joy," "Make Beauty," etc.

These are all sample questions that you may wish to ask or embellish upon any way you choose. Don't think you have to get through a specific number of questions or topics. Each one will take as long as it takes and could possibly lead conversations in new and unimaginable places! Go with it!

Time for dessert! Don't be afraid to ask your guests to help clear the table and prepare for dessert. Remember that your Dinner for God is *everyone's* Dinner for God.

Will you be making a special tea or perhaps coffee? While you are doing this, your guests who brought Desserts for God can prepare them and bring them to the table.

Repeat the manner of each guest introducing their dessert dish and why they chose to make it for this special occasion.

Once coffee and/or tea has been poured, pass around the desserts and enjoy!

You may continue with more of the above topics, or pick up from an interesting piece of conversation that happened earlier. Keep it going! Keep it fun! Keep it joyful!

When you see that you and your guests have had plenty to eat, this may be the time to begin sharing.

Remind them that in the invitation you sent out, a special sharing of something from their heart was encouraged.

This can be in the form of singing a song, reciting a poem, doing a dance, sharing a favorite passage from a favorite book, giving a special hand-made item, etc. The offerings can be limitless.

As the host, you may have to once again be the first to get things started. Share what you have prepared to show of yourself with your guests.

REMEMBER:

> *Enjoy yourself* while you are presenting your *unique* gift to God and your guests! Revel in the *knowing* that you are *loved* and *supported* while doing so! This is yet another chance for you to shine brightly for *All* that you *Are*!

> You are also setting the tone for your other guests, who will follow you in their presentations to do so without inhibition. You may have to remind them of this as well.

> After you have shown your presentation, ask your guests to present what they have chosen to share with God and the others.

> Make sure to keep it *FUN* and full of *Divine Life*!

NOTE: *If the area where you are dining is not conducive for your presentation area, go ahead and lead your guests to the area you have chosen for your God Sharing.*

Back To The Table

Once all of your guests, who have chosen to present another "God side" of themselves are done, ask everyone to return to their seats at the table.

Let the conversation go in any direction it naturally follows.
Let this be the time where *YOU* look and listen carefully to your invited guests, and be especially aware of your surroundings. Let yourself delight in the night that YOU created. Allow yourself the accolades that you truly deserve. What you have accomplished is rare, and you are in a place where you can see it taking place right in front of your very eyes! Hold the moment as close to your heart as you possibly can! You are in *Your Time*...you are in *God Time!*

When you feel the time is right…perhaps when the conversation seems to be naturally getting quieter, ask your guests for one "Final God Thought." This is an opportunity for you and your guests to give one last insight into what they might have gleaned from this profound evening.

In the story of "Dinner for God," the main character, Jenny, begins an impromptu ritual where she gives her final thoughts about her experience of the evening, then completes her account by declaring the word, "Bless." She then placed a single blue M&M from "God's dessert plate" into her mouth and savored the delicious flavor before passing the plate to her other guests, who were invited to give their closing thoughts and repeat the custom.

You may want to do something similar, or completely different. If you decide to choose a ceremony such as this, choose what you will be eating. Will it be an M&M? Perhaps you will choose a plate of toasted almonds… or another favorite delicacy.

You may choose not to pass around any sort of small edible and instead decide to simply give your final thoughts and then ask each guest to do so as well. There is no wrong way to do this.

When each person has finished giving their Final God Thoughts, ask your guests to join you in a closing meditation (or prayer). Simply ask your guests to close their eyes and go within their own Beings to acknowledge their gratitude for the special evening, to the other guests, and to the collective divine experience in which everyone participated.

Allow this silent meditation to take its own time. When you feel you are finished, open your eyes and wait for your other guests to do the same.

You may now announce that your Dinner for God has been completed.

Allow your guests to help you clean up the table, wash the dishes, and put your dining room back in order. As you have stated at the beginning, this is just as much their evening as it is God's. Participating in cleaning is just as important. Very rare will be the guest who doesn't want to help out in some way or another.

This is probably the most important part of the evening for you. (And my favorite!)

After the last of your guests have gone, give yourself the opportunity to stay in *your* moment a bit longer. This is the time where you can be aware of every single action you are making in your surroundings: Become acutely aware of each room you pass as you turn off the lights. Give one last check in the kitchen to make sure everything has been put away properly.

Perhaps you may choose to make yourself a final cup of tea, sit in God's chair, and reflect on the totality of the experience that you just created. Let your Being drink in and celebrate every waking moment of what just happened. Honor yourself for producing such an exquisite and heart-felt evening for you and your guests. Live in the pure joy and ecstasy of this quiet time.

Know that *YOU* started an occurrence that will undoubtedly excite and inspire your guests far beyond what you could possibly imagine.

YOU threw a small "God Stone" into the "Universal Waters" and caused a very *large* and *significant* wave of endless ripples of Joy and Light throughout time and space!

YOU did this…and it was *GOOD*!
It was *GOD*!

BLESS

CONGRATULATIONS!!! Hug yourself HERE!

"This is what a HUG looks like to me."

(Then make a mental note to hug yourself at least once a day for the rest of your life!)

You are undoubtedly floating on a cloud about now, yes?
And so you SHOULD!

This next section of your experience with your Dinner for God is for you to write at your leisure. Take your time. Write down what you wish in these next few pages as it comes to you. Some of it, you may want to keep fresh in your mind and put it down immediately.

Or, did you choose someone else to say "Grace?"
Why did you choose them, and what did they say?

What about dessert items? What did they bring, and why did they choose to make their special dessert?

What did you present of yourself for "God Sharing?"
What was the response?

What were you feeling and observing while you were giving your "God Sharing?"

What did other guests present of themselves for
"God Sharing?"
What were the responses?

What were you feeling and observing while others were giving their "God Sharing?"

What did you choose to serve as your final delicacy for the "Final God Thoughts?"

What did you say for your "Final God Thoughts?"

What did other people say for their "Final God Thoughts" that touched your heart?

What was the "Closing Meditation" like for you? What did you experience then?

What were some of the treasured comments you remember as your guests were leaving?

Did you sit in God's chair when everyone left? What were some of the thoughts that were going through you then?

As the evening you created is a treasured one, it's only natural to want to savor every moment of it as much as possible. No doubt your guests will feel the same way. So make sure that you share your recipes!

If you thought ahead to ask each guest who brought a dish to bring a copy of their recipe to share, that's great!

If not, this next step can be just as joy-FULL and allows a reconnection with them individually for a one-on-one recap.

Wait for a couple of days, even up to one to two weeks if you wish. Then begin contacting each of your guests in any way you choose...by phone, meeting for coffee, over lunch, etc. Ask them for the recipe of their dish and promise to make copies of all of the dishes for all of the guests who attended.

In so doing, you will most certainly reminisce about the amazing evening that you created.

What "after thoughts" did they have? What suggestions did they make?

The next few pages are designed to name your guest, the dish they brought, what observations they had, and a blank page upon which you can adhere their recipe.

Guest #1: (name):

Dish:

Their "God" experience of the evening:

_______________'s Recipe

Guest #2: (name):

Dish:

Their "God" experience of the evening:

_______________'s Recipe

Guest #3: (name):

Dish:

Their "God" experience of the evening:

__________________'s Recipe

Guest #4: (name):

Dish:

Their "God" experience of the evening:

_________________'s Recipe

Guest #5: (name):

Dish:

Their "God" experience of the evening:

______________'s Recipe

Guest #6: (name):

Dish:

Their "God" experience of the evening:

________________'s Recipe

Guest #7: (name):

Dish:

Their "God" experience of the evening:

________________'s Recipe

Guest #8: (name): _______________________

Dish: _______________________

Their "God" experience of the evening: _______________________

____

____

____

____

____

____

____

____

____

____

____

____

____

____

____

____

____

____

_______________'s Recipe

Guest #9: (name):

Dish:

Their "God" experience of the evening:

________________'s Recipe

Guest #10: (name):

Dish:

Their "God" experience of the evening:

_________________'s Recipe

Guest #11: (name):

Dish:

Their "God" experience of the evening:

_________________'s Recipe

Guest #12: (name): ______________________________

Dish: ____

Their "God" experience of the evening: ______________

____

____

____

____

____

____

____

____

____

____

____

____

____

____

____

______________'s Recipe

Now it's *your* turn! Let some time pass before you write these final pages of your magnificent experience—a couple of weeks, perhaps a month, maybe two.

Give yourself some time to let the entire evening sink in. Replay parts of it in your mind. Or mentally go through the evening step by step again. Refer back to these pages to help jog your memory. Let yourself be free with all of your thoughts and emotions as you do this.

What does it feel like to you now?

What were your favorite parts of the whole evening?

What would you have done differently?

What *wouldn't* you change a moment of?

How do you feel as you write out your experience?

These final blank pages are for you to ponder and imagine what God would say about the dinner that you created. You can choose to write this down as if you are imagining what God might say.

For example:

"God was so thrilled with the evening and the guests I chose to invite. I could see God laughing and grinning as we each talked about what Heaven looked like to us..."

Or you may choose to write it as if you have taken dictation of God's response in a more formal tone:

"The other night I had the pleasure of attending a dinner in My honor. I must say I was more than pleased with the turnout of some of my most beautiful Beings, who were splendidly dressed. It was truly a sight to behold. I especially was impressed with the dessert selection..."

Or (this one's my favorite), go ahead and put *yourself* behind God's pen and write it directly from God's point of view—*your* point of view:

"I just had the best night with some of the best Beings I've ever put on this planet! It was a dinner in MY honor! The table was incredibly beautiful, with the most delectable food that I will not soon forget! Aunt Netty's apple crisp was to die for! And the conversation was stellar! And to top it off, they gave the most amazing gifts of their talents...I don't think I ever stopped smiling..."

Make this enjoyable for yourself as you let yourself truly feel what God thought about your putting together such an amazing evening.

Use this page to sum up the entire experience of this book.

It doesn't have to be long...just a couple of affirmative statements on your completion of such an important night.

For example:

"I created a Dinner for God. I am so Blessed and Grateful that the people I invited chose to take this journey with me. It was a very profound experience, which I will think back on often—and I am most certain that I will do another one! Maybe next time I will do a Brunch for God..."

You have completed an enormous, creative task, Dear Being!

This book is now a unique "memory book" for yourself that can be referred to often. When and if you decide to have another sort of Meal for God, this can once again be your guide.

Treasure this Dinner for God Planner for yourself. Consider it as a "High Source Scrapbook!" Know that you are in every page. Look what you created! Let other people borrow it for inspiring them to have a similar experience. Pass it on to your children or other loved ones some day.

Realize that your hosting a unique dining experience such as this created a far bigger *grand* and *cosmic* wave out into the Universe than you could ever imagine!

May you also appreciate the fact that any movement that you make on a daily basis has the same effect out in the ether—you just pushed it out a little farther.

Celebrate this moment! Celebrate now! Celebrate *you* for all that you are and all that you continuously transform yourself to *Be!*

~ Be Good to Yourself ~

~ Be GOD to Yourself ~

~ *Acknowledgements* ~

A gravy ladle full of THANK YOU to my publisher and friend, Tanya Stockton from Publishing Unleashed who listens to my creative ideas and instantly tells me to 'run with it' without a moments hesitation. www.publishingunleashed.com

A serving dish of GRATITUDE to Stephanee Killen at Integrative Ink for her wise and concise editing and formatting. This planner wouldn't be nearly as exquisite without her. www.integrativeink.com

A big soup tureen of PRAISE to Barron Henzel of Henzel Design for yet again, another stellar book cover design. He never fails to take my description and turn it into something far greater than I could ever imagine! www.henzeldesign.com

A deep-dish full of heart-felt ADMIRATION to Linda Nelson for her wonderful photography skills and making me look the best I can be.

And a big platter full of APPRECIATION to you, dear reader, for making "Dinner for God" such a success and inspiring me, at your request, to make available creative tools for you to turn to time and time again for making your Dinner for God just as grand…and grander than any story I could ever tell. This is my wish for you.   Fly, dear Beings!

More information at: www.dinnerforgod.com

RAYME SCIARONI
Author, Composer, Lyricist, Theatrical Director, Designer, Artist

Following the overwhelming success of his first novel, "Dinner for God", Rayme quickly responded to readers' desires for a workbook/journal to easily guide them in planning their very own Dinner for God.

While preparing the "Dinner for God Planner", Rayme enthusiastically toured the country appearing at various events such as book signings and readings to church groups in Colorado, book clubs throughout San Diego, individual meetings of inspiration in New York City, and guest speaker at a retreat for hospital administrators in Orange County, CA.

Since authoring "Dinner for God", Rayme continued his other passions, including music writing, directing, choreographing and performing. A musical review called "The Gym" was performed in Nashville, TN ~ soon to be produced in the Greater San Diego, CA area. His direction and choreography of musical productions for the nationally known professional San Diego Junior Theatre continues to break his previous box office records. Rayme performed his co-created show of "The Needemann Brothers", at the popular "Triad" cabaret room in New York City. As pianist, he joined with some of the finest orchestras in San Diego for professional productions of "White Christmas" and "Chicago".

Rayme is overjoyed to experience so many others who appreciate and acknowledge the timely, and healing message which unfolds when participating in a Dinner for God.

Explore the fun and thoughtful following of Dinner for God fans on

~ Facebook: Dinner for God fan page ~

and

~ Twitter: DinnerforGod ~

See you there!

Rayme remains steadfast with his advice to readers:

"Be Good to Yourself ~ Be GOD to Yourself".

"Dinner for God" is now available on Amazon, Kindle, Nook, and Audible.com.

19946288R00127

Made in the USA
Charleston, SC
19 June 2013